AMAZING SCIENCE FACTS FOR KIDS

An Ideas Book for Curious Girls and Boys

ADAM KIM

Introduction

People keep saying 'science doesn't know everything'. Well, science doesn't know everything; otherwise it would stop.

Dara Ó Briain

This is a collection of science related facts that have been collected by the author which he considers amazing or surprising. It is a small fraction of the untold number of things which are astonishing, if we only decide to look carefully.

This book does not seek to explain everything about anything. It merely seeks to whet your appetite to research further something which you may find particularly interesting.

Some of the things I have mentioned have very complicated explanations. That does not mean understanding it is permanently beyond you. The most complex ideas are reached by a series of small steps, like climbing up a tall building. There is no elevator to knowledge.

If you find something that you think is amazing that you think should be included in this book, or

indeed if you believe that something is wrong in the book, then I would love to hear from you. You can email me at *blueyonderbooks@gmail.com*

I hope you enjoy the book and feel inspired to research further.

If you add a handful of salt to a glass of water the volume decreases. It becomes denser.

Cat pee glows in the dark. If a UV light is shone on it, then it will glow very brightly because it contains phosphorus.

One of the fastest man-made objects of all time is a manhole cover. In 1957 during nuclear bomb tests in Nevada a manhole cover was placed at the end of a shaft above the bomb. It reached a speed of 125,000 mph.

Dry ice is solid carbon dioxide.

Mars is easily identifiable by its reddish colour in the night sky. It is caused by it having a surface of ferric oxide. Mars has gone rusty.

Vanilla flavoring is sometimes made with the urine of beavers. I wonder who the first person to try this was.

A study has shown that blowing out the candles on a birthday cake can increase the bacteria on the cake by 1400%.

It is estimated that bacteria make up 15% of the global biomass.

A teaspoon of soil contains more microorganisms than there are people on the planet.

Your blood will travel around your body three times every minute. In a day it will travel over 12,000 miles.

When Helium is cooled to just a few degrees above absolute zero, which is minus 273.15° Celsius, then it becomes a liquid known as a superfluid. This means it can flow without friction. It can climb up and out of a glass, and when stirred continues indefinitely.

Raindrops fall at a speed of around 10 mph.

There is a liquid that you can breathe in called perfluorohexane. Animals can be submerged in a bath of oxygenated perfluorohexane without drowning.

There are one billion nanoseconds in a second.

Hawaii is moving closer to Alaska by approximately 3 inches per year due to the movement of tectonic plates.

Grasshoppers hear with their abdomens, which is where their hearing organs are located.

Fossils of grasshoppers have been found which are over 300 million years old, which is long before dinosaurs appeared.

Lobsters have blood which turns blue when exposed to oxygen because of a pigment in the blood which contains copper.

Starfish do not have a brain.

The tallest mountain in the solar system is Olympus Mons, which is an extinct volcano on Mars. It is 72,000 feet high, which is more than three times as high as Mt Everest.

An inch of rain will produce 10 inches of snow if it is cold enough to snow.

Light travels at 186,282 miles per second. A light year is the distance that light travels in one year. It is 6 trillion miles per year.

In 2009, the famous physicist Stephen Hawking held a reception for time travelers but didn't publicize it until after the event. That way, only those who could time travel would be able to attend. Sadly, nobody turned up.

If you are concerned about being abducted by aliens, then you can insure yourself against it. There have apparently been 50,000 such policies taken out, mostly in the USA and UK. There are no reports of successful claims.

John Lasseter, who became the Chief Creative Officer of Pixar was fired from Disney for promoting computer animation. Disney now owns Pixar and Lasseter is Chief Creative Officer of Disney.

A team of physicists in Australia took a photograph of the shadow of an atom, which is the smallest thing ever photographed. It is 0.4 millionth of a millimetre.

Giraffes have seven bones in their necks which is the same as humans.

Mercury is a liquid at room temperature. As mercury is nearly twice as heavy as iron you could walk on liquid mercury if you could maintain your balance.

Skipper butterflies can fly as quick as a thoroughbred horse can run. They can reach speeds of 37 mph.

MyDoom is a computer worm affecting Microsoft and first seen in 2004. It became the fastest-spreading virus ever created. The total damage done by MyDoom is estimated at $38 billion.

People with chromesthesia "see" color in sounds.

The world's tallest grass is the Dragon Bamboo. The tallest specimen was 136 feet in India.

The only rock that can float is pumice. This rock is formed from frothy lava which cools very rapidly and traps air bubbles in it.

If you put your thumb and index finger together then the distance from the top of the thumb to the top of the index finger is the same length as your nose.

In 1669 Hennig Brand accidentally discovered phosphorous while trying to turn urine into gold.

Your chances of dying on the way to get a lottery ticket are greater than your chances of winning the lottery.

Humans share 98% of their DNA with a chimpanzee, 90% with a cat and 60% with a banana.

The Eiffel tower is 6 inches taller in the summer due to metal expansion in the heat.

As we know, the earth is spinning. The circumference of the earth at the equator is about 24,901 miles. This means that if you are stood on the equator, you travel 24,901 miles in 24 hours, which is 1,038 mph.

The earth is also travelling around the sun. The approximate speed the earth goes around the sun is 1,100 miles per minute.

As well as standing on a spinning earth and the earth orbiting the sun, there is also the fact that the solar system orbits around the center of the milky way. It takes 230 million years to do a complete orbit at a speed of 515,000 mph.

The tallest tree in the world is a sequoia called Hyperion in The Redwood National Park in California. It was measured at 380.3 feet.

The largest sequoia trees transport about 500 of water in gallons up their trunks each day.

Thomas Edison, the inventor of the first practical light bulb and phonograph, filed 1,093 patents.

The oldest known living thing on earth is a Bristlecone Pine. The oldest has a verified age of 4,854 years and is called Methuselah. It is in the Inyo National Forest, Eastern California.

An octopus has 3 hearts, 9 brains and blue blood.

Bananas don't have seeds in them because they have been selectively bred not to. The most common variety is the Cavendish which was bred in 1836.

The greenhouse gas carbon dioxide makes up just 0.04% of the atmosphere.

There are 412 parts per million of carbon dioxide in the atmosphere. Between 1750 and 1800 the average concentration was 278 parts per million. NASA say that average global temperature has risen by 1.1° Celsius since 1800.

For every 512,000 human births there is one set of triplets.

There are over 43,000 different types of spiders in the world. Only 27 of these types have been known to be responsible for the death of a human.

An iceberg is always 89% submerged. The reason ice floats is because water is unusual in that it expands when frozen (which is why pipes burst in freezing weather). This means that ice is less dense than water and floats.

Usain Bolt holds the world record for the fastest 100 metres in 9.58 seconds. If Usain was unwise enough to jump off a 100 metre building it would take him 4.52 seconds to hit the floor. He would be traveling at 99 mph as he hit the ground.

There are over 200 viruses that are known to cause the common cold.

Oxygen is a colorless gas which makes up 21% of the air we breathe. However, when it becomes a liquid or a solid at very low temperatures it appears pale blue.

Polyethylene terephthalate is a plastic that is commonly used for plastic bottles. It takes 450 years to fully decompose.

You might think that the air around you doesn't weigh anything, but this is not true. A cubic metre of air, that is 1 metre high by 1 metre wide by 1 metre long, weighs 1.25 kg.

The total weight of air on Earth is 5.5 quadrillion tons (5.5 followed by 15 zeros). That is roughly one millionth of the Earth's mass.

The sea is made up of 3.5% salt. The saltiest sea is the Dead Sea in Israel which is 34% salt.

A galaxy is a massive cluster of stars, and our galaxy is called the Milky Way. It is estimated that there are 100 million stars in the Milky Way.

It is estimated that there are 2 trillion galaxies in the universe.

If we multiply the number of stars in the Milky Way by the number of galaxies, we get an estimate for the number of stars in the universe. That number is 200 billion trillion stars, or 200,000,000,000,000,000,000,000.

There are more stars than grains of sand on all the beaches in the world.

The Fermi Paradox was first posed by Enrico Fermi, an American physicist. It asks the question that seeing that life is so apparently abundant, and there are an enormous number of stars out there which could support life, why haven't we seen any evidence of aliens?

When the dinosaurs existed, there were volcanoes on the moon.

Absolute zero is the theoretical minimum temperature at which atoms stop moving. It is minus 273.15° Celsius. Surprisingly, scientists in Germany achieved a temperature of 38 trillionths of a degree above absolute zero.

If you point your car keys at your head, it increases the range of the remote signal. It does this by using your brain as a radio transmitter.

Despite being the hottest planet in the solar system it snows on Venus. The only difference is that it snows metal. The mountains are capped with two types of metal – galena and bismuthinite.

Another oddity with Venus is that a day is longer than a year. It takes about 243 Earth days to spin once, but only 225 Earth days to go all the way around the sun.

Adult cats only meow at humans and not at other cats. Kittens will meow to their mother, but they stop meowing to other cats as they get older. Perhaps it indicates how cats view us.

The French physicist, mathematician and inventor Blaise Pascal created the first roulette wheel in 1655. He was not trying to create a casino game but a perpetual motion machine.

If we expect something to occur once in 5,000 trials, a 1 in a 5,000 shot, that does not mean that it will occur once every 5,000 trials. It could be more, or it could be less. There is a 37% chance that it won't happen at all in 5,000 trials.

The mongoose is famous for killing and eating snakes. Their blood contains a protein that neutralizes snake venom.

Eating too much polar bear liver can be lethal due to overdosing on vitamin A.

The average full stop would contain about 2 million hydrogen atoms.

The first 1 GB hard drive was announced by IBM in 1980. It had a price tag of $40,000.

Off the coast of Western Australia is an island called Middle Island. This island has a 15 ha lake on it which is notable because it is a bright bubble gum pink.

North Sentinel is an island in the Bay of Bengal, off India. The indigenous Sentinelese people of this island have never been colonized, and violently repel any intruders. Several intruders have been killed. They are protected by the Indian government, and it is illegal to go within 5 miles of the island to protect the Sentinelese from infectious diseases. They live in voluntary isolation.

Tsunamis are giant waves often caused by earthquakes. In 1958 at Lituya Bay, in Alaska, an earthquake measuring 7.8 on the Richter Scale displaced a huge amount of rock and caused the largest Tsunami recorded. It measured 1,720 feet (524 metres) high.

When you put a seashell to your ear to listen to the sound of the sea what you are actually hearing is the sound of blood going through your blood vessels.

On average it takes human skin 27 days to renew itself.

You have roughly 1.6 trillion skin cells and shed about 500 million a day.

Some metals burn and react with water. Potassium is so reactive it must be stored in oil to stop it reacting with the moisture in the air.

The sun is 93 million miles away from us. If a jet could fly in space, which it can't as there is no air, it would take over 20 years to get there.

The next nearest star to us is Proxima Centauri which is a red dwarf star. It is 4 light years away, or 24 trillion miles.

Chalk comes from the shells of small sea creatures which were formed between 60 and 100 million years ago.

The largest known meteorite impact crater is the Vredefort impact structure in South Africa. It extends to 180 – 300 km across. It was caused by an asteroid believed to be 7 – 10 miles in diameter and hit approximately 2 billion years ago.

Only one person is recorded as being hit by a meteorite. In 1954 Ann Hodges was asleep on her couch when a meteorite came through her roof, bounced off the radio, and hit her on the thigh. She was fine but there was a legal dispute with her landlady as to who owned the rock.

We use wheels because they reduce friction. They are a lot easier than dragging things across the floor.

Stomach ulcers are commonplace and were thought to be the result of stress. Australian physician Barry Marshall believed that they were in fact caused by a bacteria. To prove his point, he drank a culture of the bacteria and duly developed an ulcer, which he cured with antibiotics. He shared the 2005 Nobel Prize for Medicine for his discovery.

The human skeleton repairs and renews itself every 10 years. Your bones will be made of different material in 10 years' time.

The QWERTY keyboard was invented not to be efficient but to be inefficient. The problem was that the keys jammed on the first typewriters if people typed too quickly, and QWERTY slowed the typing down. A more efficient system is the Dvorak keyboard which requires less movements, but it hasn't replaced the old keyboard.

The sun is not on fire as we understand it here on Earth as no oxygen is involved. It is a different process called nuclear fusion which requires very high temperatures and pressures.

The first photograph ever shot was in 1826, 'View from the window at Le Gras'. It took 8 hours of exposure.

Every 100 years, the moon adds approximately 1.4 milliseconds to a day. When dinosaurs were alive, days were 23 hours long, according to NASA.

An ant can't die from falling.

Helium behaves unlike any other element in that it remains a liquid at absolute zero at normal pressures. Once a pressure of 25 atmospheres is applied it will solidify.

An object in orbit is subject to gravity but is constantly falling. However, the momentum of the object balances gravity and allows it to stay in orbit. At an altitude of 150 miles an object will need a velocity of about 17,000 mph to stay in orbit. The higher the object the less the necessary velocity because gravity is reduced.

An astronaut in orbit does not experience weightlessness due to zero gravity. He will experience it because he is constantly falling.

Marie Curie's notebooks are still radioactive after 100 years. Researchers opening the lead lined boxes must wear protective clothing and sign a waiver of liability.

A cat's front paws have five toes whereas its back feet have four toes.

When you remember an event in the past you are not remembering the event but the last time you remembered it. The memory can become less precise each time you remember it to the point of being false.

If you have a ticklish throat, then scratching your ear could cure it.

Space is completely silent. Space is a vacuum; therefore sound waves will have no medium to travel through. So, it is true that in space no one will hear you scream, as the Alien movie trailer says.

The Fulgates are a family who live at Troublesome Creek, Kentucky. Remarkably they had blue skin. This is thought to be the result of a combination of inbreeding and a rare genetic condition known as methemoglobinemia.

Stomach acid has a pH of between 1 and 2 and can dissolve metal. Your stomach lining is replaced every four days to stop the acid burning through it.

The pH scale to test for alkalinity or acidity was invented by the Danish biochemist Soren Sorensen working in the Carlsberg beer laboratories in 1909.

The brain cannot feel pain as there are no pain receptors in the brain.

Hummingbirds are the only bird that can fly backwards. They can do this because of their unusual wing structure.

A moonbow is a rare nighttime rainbow.

Seahorse males get pregnant.

If you could drive a car straight up it would take about an hour to reach space as 62 miles from Earth is defined as space.

Galileo Galilei invented the thermometer in 1592.

The first Nobel Prize in physics was won by Wilhelm Rontgen for (accidentally) discovering X Rays in 1901. He donated the prize money for research and did not seek patents for his discoveries, as he believed they should be publicly available.

The wingspan of a Boeing 747 is longer than the Wright Brothers first flight.

The giant squid has the largest eyes on the planet. They are 15 inches.

Research suggests that blue, green, and hazel eyes all exist thanks to a genetic mutation. Brown was the only eye colour present in humans until about 10,000 years ago.

Koalas sleep for 18 – 22 hours a day.

The short nose bandicoot has a gestation period of 11 days whereas a female African Elephant carries its offspring for 22 months.

There are 600 muscles in the human body but over 40,000 muscles in an elephant's trunk.

Japanese scientists have revived microbes that have been in a dormant state on the South Pacific seabed for 100 million years.

Gravity varies depending where you are on earth because of mountains and the bulge in the earth at the equator. For example, gravity is 9.764 m/s^2 in Peru and 9.834 m/s^2 in the Arctic.

If you were able to drill a tunnel straight through the Earth and jumped in, it would take you exactly 42 minutes and 12 seconds to get to the other side.

Butterflies taste through their feet. Just as we have receptors on our tongue to taste butterflies have chemoreceptors on their feet.

Several animals can see ultraviolet light including butterflies, bees, birds, cats, dogs and reindeer.

Neurons send and receive signals from your brain. It is estimated that the human brain has 86 billion neurons. A fly brain has an estimated 100,000 neurons.

During the first few years of life, the brain forms more than 1 million new connections between the neurons every second.

A human baby's brain can treble in size in its first year.

Some butterflies hear with their wings.

Albert Einstein was not able to speak till he was three years old.

Monarch butterflies are the only insect that migrate to a warmer climate. They fly up to 2,500 miles from the USA and Canada to Mexico.

A jellyfish doesn't have a brain.

Jellyfish are considered biologically immortal. They don't age and will never die unless they are killed.

Jellyfish have been on earth for over half a billion (500 million) years.

Normal vision for people is 20/20. A hawk's vision is equivalent to 20/5. This means the hawk can see from 20 feet what most people can see from 5 feet.

Goats have rectangular pupils. Cuttlefish have w shaped pupils.

Most things turn to a liquid or a gas as they are heated. An egg solidifies as it is heated up.

Just over 10% of people are left handed. However, 40% of these left handed people are right footed, whereas only 3% of right handed people are left footed.

The brain's overall size begins to shrink when you're in your 30s or 40s, and the rate of shrinkage increases once you reach age 60.

The Giant Anteater has no teeth.

If the Earth were flat, on a dark night, people with perfect vision could see a candle flame flickering up to 30 miles away.

Koko, a western lowland gorilla, was taught sign language and could use 1,000 signs according to The Gorilla Foundation.

Leonardo Da Vinci described the first contact lens with a water filled glass hemisphere in 1508.

Thomas Edison invented an electric pen in 1876 that was later adapted to become the first tattoo machine in 1891.

The Empire State Building took 410 days to complete and was the world's tallest building from 1931 to 1970.

If there is a disease which is known to affect 1 in a thousand people, and there is a test for this disease which is 99% accurate, then each positive test has a 90% chance of being wrong. There will be 10 false positives for every correct positive.

You may not quite see your face like this, but it is a biological crumple zone. If you fall flat on your face it helps to avoid damage to the brain by absorbing the shock.

The magnetic North Pole is moving. It is different to the actual North Pole and is in northern Canada. It is moving towards Russia at a speed of 34 – 37 miles per year.

There is one planet that we know is populated entirely by robots – Mars.

We often think that bones are inside us, in reality the opposite is true. Our brain is within our skull.

Our nearest neighboring galaxy, the Andromeda Galaxy, is going to crash into our Milky way galaxy in 4.5 billion years. The Andromeda Galaxy has about 1 billion stars and the Milky Way has about 100 million. A collision between two stars is highly unlikely because of the huge distances between stars.

The Andromeda Galaxy is approaching us at 68 miles a second.

The nearest star to us is Proxima Centauri which is 4.2 light years away. If our sun was the size of a ping pong ball, then Proxima Centauri would be the size of a pea and 680 miles away.

Have you ever wondered why toast browns? It is a chemical reaction between amino acids and reducing sugars which give it a distinct flavor. It is called a Maillard Reaction.

The lowest natural temperature ever recorded at ground level was at the Vostok Station in Antarctica when the temperature was recorded in July 1983 at minus 89.2° centigrade.

The Amazon rain forest is believed to be at least 55 million years old.

Toxoplasma Gondii is a parasite that can infect warm blooded animals. However, it can only reproduce in a cat. When the parasite infects rats and mice it changes their behaviour to be less frightened of cats and more explorative, thus increasing its chances of reproducing.

Mycology is the branch of botany concerned with the study of fungi. However, it is now known that fungi are genetically more closely related to animals than plants.

Ötzi the Iceman, is a natural mummy of a man who lived between 3350 and 3105 BC. He was discovered in the Alps in Austria in 1991 by some tourists. Innsbruck Medical University analysed the DNA of 3,700 Tyrolean male blood donors and found that 19 were direct descendants of Ötzi.

Angustopila psammion is the world's smallest known snail. It lives in North Vietnam and the shell measures 0.6mm. Fifteen could fit together in the eye of a needle.

Metamorphosis is one of the most remarkable processes in nature. A caterpillar will liquefy virtually all its organs during the process of becoming a butterfly or moth. A caterpillar will release an enzyme inside the chrysalis that rip apart and dissolve cells in its muscles, digestive system, and other organs. It can take as little as 16 days to transform into a butterfly.

Research was carried out into caterpillars which involved training them to associate a particular smell with receiving an electric shock. Perhaps surprisingly it was found that when the caterpillar went through metamorphosis and became the resultant adult moth, they still avoided this smell.

The first vacuum cleaner was invented in 1901 by Henry Cecil Booth. It was horse drawn as it was so large.

Some animals can reproduce by parthenogenesis, which means that females can produce offspring without a male. The largest animal with this ability is the Komodo dragon.

When glass breaks the cracks move at a speed of up to 3,000 mph.

Sound travels faster in water than air. In air it travels at 331 metres per second but in water it travels at 1,496 metres a second.

Light slows down in water.

Mach 1, which is the speed of sound, is approximately 761 miles per hour.

Scallops are a type of saltwater clam. They have a super sensitive visual system with up to 200 eyes.

Insect blood is clear or tinged with yellow or green. The red you see if you crush a midge is pigment from its eyes, or it may be your blood if it has been sucking your blood.

Flowers appeared some 140 million years ago. Before that, trees bearing cones and ferns dominated the earth.

Krakatoa is a volcanic island between Java and Sumatra. In 1883 it exploded with the loudest explosion in recorded history. It was heard in Perth which is 1930 miles away and the resultant Tsunami travelled around the world three and a half times.

A tsunami can travel at about 500 mph over open ocean. They are shallow and very long waves in the ocean but slow up in shallow water and the wave builds to create the destructive tsunami wave that we see on the news.

According to the World Health Organisation 627,000 people died of malaria in 2020.

The peacock mantis shrimp is a beautiful little creature that packs a punch. It has the fastest punch of any recorded animal at speeds of 23m/sec. The acceleration is equivalent to a bullet leaving a handgun. They have been known to break the glass of aquariums.

The founders of Google, Microsoft, Hewlett Packard, and Apple started building their computers from a garage before they were able to advance to becomes the mega companies they are today.

Owls don't have eyeballs. They have tube-like or cylindrical type shapes filled with a clear liquid that they use to see in the dark.

Normal pens work by gravity pulling the ink down to the nib as you are writing. However, in zero gravity of space this won't work. The Fisher Space Pen Company overcame this by having pressurized ink cartridges.

Zebra stripes act as a natural bug repellant. It has been found that flies are averse to landing on a black and white surface.

If you sneeze while traveling at 60 mph, your eyes are closed for an average of 50 feet.

The first webcam was created at Cambridge University in 1990. They used the webcam to watch a coffee maker, eliminating the need to make trips to an empty pot.

If you rub an onion on your foot, you'll be able to taste it within 30-60 minutes because it travels through the blood stream.

Viruses exist in the atmosphere and fall to Earth every day. Researchers at the British Columbia University found around 800 million viruses fall per square metre from the sky each day.

Human skin is a fertile environment for microbes and around 1,000 types of bacteria have been found. There are an average of 32 million bacteria per square inch of skin. It might sound creepy, but most are not only harmless but beneficial.

An average male brain has approximately 4% more cells and 100 grams more brain tissue than an average female brain. This does not mean that men are more intelligent though. Research points to no overall difference in intelligence between males and females.

Sperm whales have the biggest brains which weigh about 7.7 kg, compared to human brains which are about 1.2 kg.

Planes stay in the air because of the shape of their wings. Air moving over the wing gets forced downwards, which pushes the wing up. This push is stronger than gravity, and so makes the plane fly.

Sharks don't have any bones. They have strong flexible cartilage.

If you flip a shark upside down (not recommended) they go into a trance like state called tonic immobility.

Sharks are ancient animals. Based on fossils found in Australia and the USA scientists estimate that sharks are over 450 million years old. That is about 100 million years older than trees.

The sun is 70% hydrogen, 28% helium and 2% other mass. The sun rotates about once every 27 days.

Uranus spins on its side.

Air becomes a liquid at minus 194° Celsius.

Rats laugh when they are tickled.

Whales used to have four legs and lived on land around 50 million years ago.

Your nose is always in your field of vision, but your brain filters it out through a process called Unconscious Selective Attention.

June and Jennifer Gibbons were identical twins and grew up in Wales. They were known as "The Silent Twins" as they only communicated with each other.

A placebo is a medication which has no therapeutic effect. However, it is believed that placebos can have a positive effect on patient outcomes. It has been found that placebo's work best for women if the pill is blue and best for men if it is orange.

The recent Covid pandemic is not a new phenomenon. In 1918 the Spanish Flu pandemic is believed to have killed between 17 and 50 million people worldwide and lasted for three years. Unlike Covid the Spanish Flu pandemic killed mostly young adults. In the USA nearly half of those who died were aged 20 – 40.

The most fatal pandemic in human history was the Black Death, which was a bubonic plague pandemic, from 1346 – 1353. It is estimated to have caused the death of between 75 – 200 million people. It is likely that the disease killed 45 – 50% of the European population at the time.

Non Newtonian fluids are fluids whose viscosity changes under stress. For example, when you shake a ketchup bottle it becomes runnier because it is a non-Newtonian fluid. Other examples include corn starch, custard, and paint.

If you fold a piece of paper in half, you double its thickness. The average piece of paper is about 0.004 inches thick. If you could fold it ten times, it would make it roughly the thickness of your hand. If you could fold it 23 times, the thickness increases to a kilometre. If you fold it 51 times you will reach the sun, and you'll get a piece of paper larger than the observable universe with 103 folds. It is only possible to do 8 folds though.

Adult Mayflies have no mouth.

Lead can be changed into gold. However, the process which involves a particle accelerator is far too expensive to be economic.

The hardest substance in the human body is tooth enamel.

Betelgeuse is a red supergiant star which is roughly 950 times bigger than our star. Betelgeuse is on the point of transitioning from a supergiant to a supernova, and this is expected to happen any time in the next 100,000 years. When it does it would light our sky continuously for two months, despite being 500 – 600 light years away.

Despite being massive Betelgeuse is not the largest star that has been located though. The largest is known as UY Scuti and is 1700 times bigger than our sun. If it were at the centre of our solar system, its edge would extend beyond the orbit of Jupiter.

There is enough salt in the oceans to cover all the land to a depth of 500 feet.

The typical brain comprises about 2% of the body's total weight but uses 20% of its total energy and oxygen intake.

A neuron or nerve cell communicates to other cells via synapses. A piece of brain tissue the size of a grain of sand contains 100,000 neurons and 1 billion synapses, all communicating with each other.

Each neuron can transmit 1,000 nerve impulses per second and make tens of thousands of synaptic contacts with other neurons.

The Scoville Heat Test was developed in 1912 as a measurement of the spiciness of chili peppers. It was a subjective test based on the evidence of people experienced in eating chilis. It has been replaced with more objective analytical techniques.

When you cut an onion, it releases sulfur based chemicals which reacts with your tear film on your eyes creating sulfuric acid. This is what makes you cry. It can be avoided if you wear goggles while cutting the onions.

The sun has a circumference of 2,713,406 miles while the Earth's circumference is 24,901 miles. Approximately one million earths could fit inside the sun.

Each second the sun converts 700 million tons of the element hydrogen into 695million tons of the element helium. The sun loses about 5.5 million tons of mass every second. This is given off as energy in the form of gamma rays.

Protaxites are a form of fungi that has been found in the fossil record dating to about 400 million years ago. They formed trunk like structures 1 metre (3 feet) wide and 8 metres (26 feet) high.

Sound travels two to three times faster through helium than it does through air. This is why inhaling helium makes your voice higher.

When the moon was first formed, about 4.5 billion years ago, it is estimated that it orbited 14,000 miles away from the Earth, compared to 250,000 miles today. The moon being so close resulted in a day being only 5 hours long.

The moon is moving away from the earth at 3.78cm (1.48 inches) per year. This is measured by laser reflectors which were left on the moon by astronauts during the Apollo moon mission.

The bread slicing machine was invented by Otto Rohwedder, an American inventor from Iowa. The sliced bread produced first went on sale on 7th July 1928 at the Chillicothe Baking Company, in Missouri.

Lightning strikes produce ozone, which adds to the ozone layer. That is why some thunderstorms smell of ozone.

The word laser is an acronym for light amplification by stimulated emission of radiation. The first laser was built in 1960 by Theodore Maiman, an American engineer and physicist.

The largest spider is the Goliath Birdeater from South America. It can weigh 175g and has a leg span of up to 30cm (12 inches). It is big enough to cover a dinner plate.

March 14th is Save a Spider Day in the USA.

Charles Babbage built a model of the first mechanical computer in 1822.

Ada Lovelace was a mathematician and accepted as being the first computer programmer when she published an algorithm for Charles Babbage's calculating machine. She was the first to realise that Babbage's machine had applications beyond pure calculation. She was born on the 10th December 1815

It is possible to break a rib if you sneeze hard enough.

Plastic is made from crude oil and gas which is in turn created by the fossils of plants and tiny marine organisms.

At present the atmosphere is made up of 21% oxygen. At the end of the carboniferous period, which was about 300 million years ago, the atmosphere had 35% oxygen.

Waving a red towel at bulls doesn't make them angry. They are completely color blind.

If you cut a starfish, it won't bleed because it doesn't have any blood. Instead, they use seawater to circulate nutrients around their body.

The whale shark is the largest fish in the sea and can grow over 60 feet. They feed on plankton which consist of some of the smallest organisms in the oceans.

Many plankton are bioluminescent, which means that they can light up. They do this by mixing certain chemicals together which produce a flash of light. This is believed to be a defensive mechanism as the flash of light may attract a predator to whatever is disturbing the plankton.

So far, two diseases have successfully been eradicated: smallpox and rinderpest. The last case of smallpox was in 1977, and the last of rinderpest was in 2001.

If you mix half a litre of water and half a litre of alcohol, then the resultant mixture will be less than a litre.

Bee stings are acidic and wasp stings are slightly alkaline. Bee stings can be treated by neutralising the acid with a mild alkali, such as bicarbonate of soda. Wasp stings can be treated by neutralising with an acid, such as vinegar. It is important to know what has stung you.

DNA is flame retardant. It is unclear why this is or if there are any useful implications.

Hydrogen makes up 62% of the atoms in the human body. These hydrogen atoms were formed 13.7 billion years ago in the Big Bang.

Frogs do not need to drink using their mouths. The absorb water through their skin.

Copper has antibacterial properties. It can prevent bacteria and germs from spreading. It has been used for hospital door handles and water pipes for many years for this reason.

Copper is the most recycled metal. It is estimated that 80% of the copper ever mined is still in use.

Gallium is a silvery metal at a room temperature of 25° Celsius. However, if you hold it in your hands it will melt as the melting point of gallium is 30° Celsius and your body temperature is 37° Celsius.

If liquid gallium is poured on an aluminum sheet odd things start to happen. The gallium infiltrates the crystal structure of the aluminum and turns the aluminum into a very weak alloy.

Halley's Comet is the only comet that is visible to the naked eye and can appear twice in a lifetime. It last appeared in 1986 and will next appear in mid 2061.

The appearance of Halley's Comet in 1910 created some hysteria and doomsday predictions. Two enterprising Texas men were selling some anti-comet pills. They were arrested but their clients rioted till they were released.

Some people can hear their eyeballs moving in their eye sockets. The muscles that move the eyes are connected to the bones of the skull and there is a small amount of friction as these muscles move. Some people can detect that friction as a noise in their ear. This condition is said to affect 1 in 500,000 people.

Snowflakes fall at approximately 1.5 mph. On average they travel for 45 minutes before hitting the ground.

The oceans are 12,080 feet deep on average. The deepest point is the Mariana Trench in the Pacific Ocean which is over 35,000 feet at its deepest.

A day on Mars lasts for 24 hours 39 minutes and 35 seconds. As this is more than an Earth day you might assume from that bit of information that there are less Martian days in a year than Earth days. You would be wrong though. Mars takes 687 Earth days to orbit the sun during which time there are 672 Martian days.

Lomatia tasmanica is an unusual plant from Tasmania. Although the plant produces bright red flowers in the summer it cannot reproduce from seeds as they are sterile. It has to reproduce vegetatively by dropping branches that root to produce a new plant. There are believed to be only 300 plants left in the wild.

ENIAC (Electronic Numerical Integrator and Computer) was developed in 1945 and was the first programmable, electronic, and general purpose digital computer. It was developed by the US military to calculate artillery firing tables. It measured 2 x 1 x 30 metres, had 5 million hand soldered joints, and weighed 27 tons.

There are 63,000 searches on google a second.

At the end of the last ice age, about 6,000 years ago, the sea level had risen about 120 metres (390 feet)

It is estimated that in adults 50 – 70 billion cells die per day. That is about 40 million per minute.

It is estimated that there are 30 trillion cells in an adult human body.

The universe was created in the Big Bang which was approximately 13.77 billion years ago.

The sun is about 4.5 billion years old. This means that the universe existed for some 9.3 billion years before our sun and solar system were formed.

Some smaller mammoths survived on Wrangel Island, which is in the Arctic Ocean, till about 4,000 years ago.

Most plants are green and generate their food from chlorophyll using the energy of sunlight. The Ghost plant (Monotropa Uniflora) does not have any chlorophyll and is white. The plant is parasitic and ultimately gets its food from photosynthesizing trees.

The American moon moth emerges into its adult winged stage with no mouthparts or digestive system and does not eat in their adult form. There sole function is to reproduce, and they rely on the energy they built up as caterpillars.

Penicillin was one of the great advances in medicine and the first widely used antibiotic. It was discovered in 1928 by Scottish physician Alexander Fleming by accident. Fleming inoculated several culture plates with a bacterium and then went on holiday, leaving the top off one. When he came back, he found that a blue green mold had contaminated it and was killing the bacterium. The rest is history.

Earth shares its orbit with an asteroid called 2010 TK7.

Sound waves can be used to levitate objects through a process called Acoustic Levitation.

The Mariana snailfish is the deepest fish found in the ocean so far. It has been found around 8,000m below the surface in the Mariana Trench. They thrive despite the massive pressure which is about 800 times atmospheric pressure at that depth.

An adult has 206 bones in their body. At birth a baby has 300 bones, many of which fuse as they get older.

Over half your bones are in your hands and feet. Each foot has 26 bones and each hand 27 bones.

The number of people working for NASA on the Apollo space project, which landed men on the moon, was about 400,000 in total.

Josephine Cochrane was the American inventor of the first commercially successful dishwasher. She said, "If nobody else is going to invent a dish washing machine, I'll do it myself". Josephine Cochrane got her patent on 28th December 1886.

The first website that went online was “info.cern.ch”. This was created by Tim Berners-Lee, the inventor of the World Wide Web, at the research lab CERN in 1990.

Caterpillars have 12 eyes.

A skydiver will reach their terminal velocity of about 122 mph after about 10 seconds. They won’t increase in speed after this because gravity and the air resistance from falling will have equal magnitude and cancel each other out.

Pistol Shrimps are one of the most extraordinary animals. Despite being only 3-5cm (1 -2 inches) long it produces one of the loudest noises measured at 218 decibels, competing with the sperm whale for the loudest animal noise. It creates this sound by snapping its claw which creates a bubble which shoots out at 62mph. This bubble reaches a temperature of 4,700° Celsius for a very short period which then implodes to produce the sound.

In a room of 35 people the probability that two of these people will have the same birthday is 85%.

The temperature of outer space is minus 270.42° centigrade. Given that absolute zero is minus 273.15° outer space is distinctly chilly. Space also has a smell. It is said to smell metallic and acrid.

The deadliest animal isn't the tiger or a shark. It is the mosquito which the World Health Organisation estimates kills about 725,000 each year through diseases such as malaria, dengue fever and yellow fever.

Using Kevlar as a bulletproof vest was invented by a pizza delivery guy Richard Davis, from Detroit USA. He developed the idea after shooting three armed assailants in self-defense during a delivery. During testing he shot himself 190 times in the chest. Davis sold the company for $45m in 2005.

Hot water freezes faster than cold water. This is known as the Mpemba effect. This is named after a Tanzanian schoolboy, Erasto Mpemba. In

1963 he discovered the phenomenon while preparing ice cream to earn pocket money.

Hot water is also heavier than cold water, because as Einstein told us $E=mc^2$. So, if E, the energy in the water, goes up because it's hotter then mass, m, must also go up to keep the equation balanced.

Everything has an inside and an outside, doesn't it? A ball, an envelope, even a cat has an inside and outside. However, a Mobius Strip only has one side. It can be created by attaching two ends of a strip of paper together with a half twist.

The sunset on Mars is blue.

The body creates about 2 million red blood cells every second. The red blood cell takes about 60 seconds to circulate around the human body. After about 100-120 days their components are recycled.

Most sharks must keep swimming, so that the water is constantly passed through their gills. If they stop, they will drown.

Time is slower at higher altitudes than at lower altitudes, by a miniscule amount. This was a theoretical proposition from Einstein's General Theory of Relativity but has now been measured with an extremely accurate atomic clock.

Carrots originally come from Afghanistan and were purple. They have been cultivated to be orange.

The collective name for Gnus is an implausibility of Gnus.

If you make ice cubes with tap water, they will be white; if you use boiled water, they will be transparent. Boiling water removes the gases in the solution prior to freezing.

The IBM 5120 from 1980 was the heaviest desktop computer ever made. It weighed about 105 pounds, not including the 130 pounds external floppy drive.

A micromort is a measure of the risk of dying from different activities measured as chances per million. This is perhaps something that we tend to gloss over in everyday life. For example, in the

UK measured over 20 years 41 people have died skydiving out of nearly 5 million jumps. That is about 8 per million, or 8 micromorts from sky diving.

Other micromorts are.

Skiing (per day)	1
Traveling 6,000 miles in a jet	1
Running a marathon	7
Getting out of bed (aged 75)	105
Climbing Mt Everest	37,932

Stonehenge was built in various phases but was begun in 3000 – 2920 BC. The Giza pyramids were built in 2550 – 2490 BC.

The average adult will inhale and exhale about 8 litres of air per minute. That is about 11,000 litres per day. Oxygen in the atmosphere is about 20% and in breath, when breathed out, 15%. Therefore 5% is consumed of the 11,000 litres which means 550 litres of oxygen are consumed by a person every day.

If the sun just happened to vanish then it would be 8 minutes and 20 seconds before we would find out. That is how long light takes to reach us from the sun.

We would also stop orbiting in 8 minutes 20 seconds because gravity travels at the speed of light.

The rate of colorblindness in women is 1 in 200 (0.5%) while in men it is 1 in 12 (8%). The reason for this disparity is that X chromosomes are responsible for color vision. You will have full color vision as long as at least one X chromosome is functioning properly. However, since men have only one X chromosome and women have two men are more likely to be colorblind.

Ants have two stomachs. One is for storing food for their own consumption, and the other is for sharing food with other ants.

On Earth, there are more trees than stars in our galaxy. There are estimated to be 100 billion stars in our galaxy, but there are also estimated to be 3 trillion trees on Earth.

The most powerful recorded volcanic eruption occurred at Mount Tambora in Indonesia in 1815.

The explosion ejected approximately 50 cubic miles of material into the atmosphere. This amount of material in the atmosphere caused global cooling of about 0.5° Celsius, and 1816 is known as the year without a summer. This cooling is estimated to have led to the deaths of 90,000 people.

The oldest spider was an Australian trap door spider called 'Number 16'. It was studied for 43 years.

Two 12 inch pizzas have less pizza than one 18 inch pizza.

During World War II the US Army wanted to reduce bomber casualties. They had data on where the most bullet holes were on each square foot of planes and wanted to armor plate the areas with the most holes. The formed a Statistical Research Group to look at the problem. They said they needed to put the armor plating where there were no bullet holes as the ones who were hit there didn't make it back. The Army's thinking is called 'Survivorship bias'. It overlooks things that are not visible.

When your mother was born, she was already carrying the egg that would become you.

There are more atoms in a glass of water than glasses of water in all the oceans.

Probability is determined by the information we have, which can seem paradoxical at times. For example;

a) If a couple have two children, and we know the eldest is a boy, then the chances of the other child being a boy is 50%.

b) However, if a couple have two children and we only know one of them is a boy, then the odds on the other being a boy is 33%. This difference is explained because there are four possible outcomes that the parents could have.

Boy – Boy
Boy – Girl
Girl – Boy
Girl – Girl

The girl – girl option is not available as they already have a boy. That leaves 2 out of 3 of the possibilities being a girl as the second child.

Encephalitis lethargica is a disease which attacks the brain. From 1915 – 1926 there was a pandemic of the disease which left an estimated 500,000 dead. The cause of the pandemic is unknown, but it mysteriously disappeared in 1927.

Several scientific studies show a direct connection between indoor tanning beds and cancer, and the World Health Organization has classified tanning beds as a Level 1 carcinogen, the same as plutonium and cigarettes.

The Earth is obviously not flat, but it's not exactly round, either. It's more of a squashed sphere, because when it spins, gravity pushes in, and centrifugal force pushes out causing a bulge around the middle.

Lene Hau is a Danish physicist and remarkably she was able to slow down the speed of light from 300,000 km a second to about 17 metres per second in 1999. In 2001 she was able to stop a beam completely. “We can hold on to the light, move it around or even save it for later. We can actually manipulate it,” says Hau.

A photon is a particle of light that the sun creates in the process of fusion reactions inside its core.

It takes a photon 40,000 years to reach the surface of the sun. It then takes approximately 8 minutes 20 seconds to reach your eyeball.

Frogs do not need to drink using their mouths. They absorb water through their skin through a process called osmosis.

The only two non-silvery metals are gold and copper.

There are more variants of a game of chess than there are atoms in the universe. The number of different games of chess is at least 10 followed by 120 zeros.

Every planet of the whole solar system could physically fit between the earth and the moon if we ignore gravity.

Those born blind experience dreams involving things such as emotion, sound and smell rather than sight.

Research suggests that 12% of people dream in black and white, and that this percentage increases with age.

Lucid dreaming is where you are aware you are dreaming while you are still asleep. During this you can control or direct your dream. About 50% of people can recall having such a dream.

The rarest element is Astatine. It is only produced as heavier metals decay and has a half-life of 8.1 hours. It is estimated that there is less than 1 gram naturally occurring in the Earth's crust at any time.

If all the blood vessels of the human body are put together, their length will reach 60,000 miles.

We have the same number of hairs on our body as a chimpanzee. The difference is not the number but that human hairs are thinner and more transparent.

Spiders have a lack of muscles in their legs. They move by pumping blood throughout their bodies and legs, and it is the pressure that allows them to move and not muscles as with us.

According to research from John Hopkins University, the average color of the universe is a shade of beige which is described as a 'cosmic latte.'

Percy Spencer was an American physicist who specialized on radars. One day he was standing in front of an active radar when he noticed the candy in his pocket had melted. He wasn't the first to notice this effect, but he was the first to investigate it. Spencer then created the first true microwave oven by attaching a high-density electromagnetic field generator to an enclosed metal box. Like many inventions, the microwave came about from an accident and a curious mind.

The company Spencer worked for, Raytheon, filed a patent for a microwave cooking oven in 1945. It went on sale in 1947 and the first commercial examples were 6 feet tall, weighed 750lbs and cost $5,000. The average annual wage was $3,000 in 1947.

Dragonflies have six legs, like other insects, but are unable to walk. They have been around for 300 million years, so it clearly hasn't restricted them much.

Dragonflies live as underwater nymphs for up to 4 years. They have gills at the base of their rectum and breathe through their bottom. When the nymph wants to move, they shoot this water out and are jet propelled forwards.

A pure element can take more than one form. For example, carbon can come in the form of diamonds, graphite, or coal.

There are 94 chemical elements that occur naturally. Six of them make up 99% of our bodies. They are oxygen, carbon, hydrogen, nitrogen, calcium, and phosphorus. Another 0.85% is composed of five more elements they are potassium, sulfur, sodium, chlorine, and magnesium. In total 60 elements make up the human body.

The gravity of the moon makes the oceans bulge and causes tides.

Objects fall with the same rate of acceleration no matter what the mass is. Galileo showed this in the 14th Century when he dropped two spheres with different masses from the Leaning Tower of Pisa.

The U.S. Department of Energy says on average, 75 percent of the electricity used to power home electronics and appliances is consumed while the products are turned off.

Have you ever wondered why sandcastles hold together better when the sand is slightly damp? The answer is water tension between the sand and water molecules. Too much or too little and it won't work.

Termite queens live longer than any other insect. They can live up to 20 years. They do this while continuously laying 20,000 eggs a day. The workers, however, live only a few months.

The Golden Dart Frog, a native of Colombia, is the most poisonous animal on the planet. The average Golden Dart Frog has enough poison to kill an estimated 10 – 20 people or two African bull elephants.

Graham's number is a very big number. It was discovered by an American mathematician Ronald Graham, while solving a problem in an area of mathematics called Ramsey Theory. Even if every digit of Graham's number was written in

the tiniest writing possible, it would be too big to fit in the observable universe.

A pigeon's feathers weigh more than their bones. Its bones are hollow and therefore very light to facilitate flight.

A glass ball will bounce higher than a rubber one, as long as it doesn't break.

Goosebumps are caused by muscles. They are a reaction to increased adrenaline when we are frightened or emotional. Although they are redundant in humans these days, they make animals seem bigger when under threat. They are a remnant from our evolutionary predecessors.

A team from North Carolina State University studied the belly buttons of 60 different people and they found a "rain forest" of microscopic life. In total, they identified 2,368 bacterial species, 1,458 of which may be new.

The cornea is part of the eye and is the only part of the body that has no blood. It gets oxygen directly from the air.

After Beethoven became deaf, he is believed to have fixed a metal rod to his piano and bit down on it while he played. This allowed him to hear the sounds perfectly through vibrations in the jawbone. It is called 'bone conduction'.

Bone conduction is also why we hear our voices differently when they are played back to us as opposed to hearing them live. The skull conducts lower frequencies better than air and people believe their voices are lower than they are as a result.

Sunflowers are what environmental scientists call hyperaccumulators. They are plants that can take up high concentrations of toxic materials and radiation in their tissues. After the Fukushima nuclear disaster, fields of sunflowers were planted across the affected landscapes to help absorb toxic metals and radiation from the soil. It may take longer than traditional methods, but it is easier to dispose of sunflowers than dig up a contaminated area.

A neutron star is a supergiant star which has collapsed and become astonishingly dense. If a matchbox contained the material from a neutron star it would weigh 3 billion tons. The gravitational field of a neutron star at the surface is about 200 billion times the Earth's.

The fastest-spinning neutron star is known as PSR J1748-2446ad and rotates at a rate of 716 times a second. If you could stand on the equator, you would be travelling at 24% of the speed of light.

Our Milky Way galaxy is 105,700 light years wide. While the Andromeda Galaxy is 220,000 light years wide.

The center region of the Milky Way is called the Galactic Center, and it contains a supermassive black hole which is about 4 million times the mass of the sun and is called Sagittarius A

If you grind a marine sponge through a sieve into salt water, it'll reorganize itself back into a sponge. It's the only animal that we know that can do that.

Humans can only sense temperature and pressure. We do not sense wetness.

African lions catch about 20% of the prey they chase. Dragonflies catch 95%. Dragonflies are the world's deadliest hunters.

The first word sent over the internet was on October 29th, 1969, by experts in Silicon Valley. The first word was meant to be 'login', but the system crashed before the word could be completed. The first word sent over the internet is therefore 'lo'.

In 1999 NASA's $327m Mars Climate Orbiter crashed into the surface of Mars before it could begin operations. The cause of the failure was a mix up between metric and imperial units which meant the craft was on the wrong trajectory.

Maurice Hilleman was a leading American microbiologist who specialized in vaccines. Of the 14 vaccines which are recommended in American vaccine schedules Hilleman and his team have developed 8 including measles, mumps, Hepatitis A and hepatitis B. It is estimated his vaccines save nearly 8 million lives a year.

A Dyson Sphere is a theoretical structure proposed by physicist Freeman Dyson in 1960.

He suggested that an advanced civilisation could build a structure to encompass a star to act as a light trap to capture solar energy. Such a structure is a long way from current capabilities, but who knows what potential alien civilisation may have done.

In 2013 Chinese scientists have successfully grown teeth from stem cells harvested from urine.

The sun generates energy by turning hydrogen into helium. As the hydrogen is gradually used up the sun will turn into a red giant. It will become bigger and brighter. This expansion is likely to reach the orbit of Mars, which means that Mercury, Venus, and the Earth will be consumed by the expanding red giant. Don't worry too much yet as this will take 5 billion years.

J Lyons and Co were one of the UK's leading food manufacturing companies. They developed the first computer for business use called LEO 1 (Lyons Electronic Office 1). The computer occupied 2,500 sq feet of office space in Hammersmith. Among its initial tasks was adding receipts for iced buns.

As is well known seawater is toxic if you drink it because the high salt content will dehydrate you and can lead to death. However, your chances are improved considerably if you eat frozen seawater as it contains only 10% of the salt that is in the liquid form.

Voyager 1 was launched in 1977 to study the solar system and interstellar space. The probe is still going strong and in interstellar space some 15 billion miles away from us. It is traveling at 38,026.77 mph, according to NASA, who have a web page detailing where and how far away the craft is. Voyager is still sending data back to Earth.

Attached to Voyager is a 'Golden Record' which is in effect an introduction to humans for any alien which may find the spacecraft. There are many things on the Golden Record including a photograph of the Golden Gate Bridge, whale song and Chuck Berry singing 'Johnny B. Goode'.

On February 14th, 1990, Voyager 1 took the famous 'Pale Blue Dot' photo of the Earth from a record distance of 3.7 billion miles. The apparent size of Earth is less than a pixel and appears as a blue dot against the vastness of space.

A severe earthquake which hit Christchurch in New Zealand in 2011 caused 185 deaths as well as the destruction of many buildings. Japanese architect Shigeru Ban, who is characterized as a 'Disaster Architect', was asked to design a replacement for the cathedral. He worked for free and designed what is known as 'The Cardboard Cathedral'. The structure rises to nearly 70 feet and uses 24 inch diameter cardboard tubes, timber, and steel.

It is believed that there are 50 million distinct species of invertebrates living in rainforests. A single tree in Peru yielded 50 different species of ants, which is the same as are in the whole of the UK.

While munching on Pringles crisps have you ever wondered what the shape of the crisp is called. Well, it is a 'Hyperbolic Paraboloid'. It was designed by Frederic Baur in 1966 who was an organic chemist. It is shaped that way so the weight of the stack of crisps won't crush the bottom crisp. He was so proud of his invention that he asked that his ashes be buried in a Pringles carton, which they were.

The Rubik's cube was invented by Hungarian Erno Rubik in 1974. It took the inventor a month to solve it. The present record for solving it is held by Feliks Zemdegs who took 4.22 seconds.

There is an opposite of albino animals, which aren't white, but black. These are known as Melanistic animals. The black panther is a melanistic jaguar.

When you exercise or are dieting, the burned fat metabolizes to become carbon dioxide, water, and energy. You breathe out the fat that you burn.

About 50% of a tree is dry matter and 47.5% of the dry matter consists of carbon. This the tree gets from carbon dioxide in the air, possibly from the fat you burned while out for a run.

If you click on Wikipedia, then you will have just got a load of data from Ashburn in Virginia where Wikipedia is based. The request has traveled from your computer through a local Wi-Fi router or a modem, up to a local data centre, from there onwards (under ocean if you're overseas), all the way to Virginia, and back again – in around 0.1 of a second, depending on how good your internet connection is.

Honey, and items immersed in honey, can be preserved for centuries. The long shelf life is due to an enzyme found in the stomachs of bees.

Nils Bohlin, a Swedish engineer working for Volvo, invented the three point seat belt in 1959. Volvo felt the development was so important for safety that they gave it away free to other car manufacturers.

It is calculated that the smartest animal, other than humans is the orangutan. This is followed in order by Bottlenose Dolphin, Chimpanzee, Elephant, African Grey Parrot, Octopus and Pig.

New research published in Animal Behaviour suggest that the smaller the animal the more information it can process in a small amount of time. That would suggest some small animals are seeing the world in slow motion. Dogs take in visual information 25% quicker than humans.

Our sense of smell is responsible for about 80% of what we taste.

Broccoli is not a natural vegetable but is man made from selective breeding of wild cabbage plants. It originated in the Northern Mediterranean around the sixth century BC.

There are smoke alarms for the deaf. One solution has been by activating strobe lighting. The most effective solution was developed by the Department of Medicine at Shiga University in Japan involves spraying wasabi extract, a type of horseradish.

Russian astronauts took a TP-82 pistol with them into space. This wasn't in case they happened across some unfriendly aliens on their trip though. It was for when they landed in Siberia in case bears or wolves found them before the rescue crews.

About 20% of all mammal species are bats. There are about 1200 species of bat.

Wildfires are a big problem in Australia. The situation is not helped by three birds, Black Kites,

Whistling Kites, and Brown Falcons. They all purposely pick up burning sticks and drop them to spread the fire in the hope of flushing out prey.

Daniel Kish is a remarkable person who is blind. He doesn't rely on a guide dog or white stick to get about. He uses echolocation, like bats. He clicks his tongue and sends out flashes of sound that bounce off surfaces in the environment and return to him, helping him to construct an understanding of the space around him.

Did you realise that eyelash mites were a thing? Well, you almost certainly have them, though they don't become a problem unless they breed exponentially which can lead to soreness.

If two pieces of the same type of metal touch in space, they will permanently bond. There is no liquid or molten phase in the joint. This is known as "cold welding" It doesn't happen on Earth because of the air and water found between the pieces.

At the start of the universe in the Big Bang there were only two elements, hydrogen and helium.

All the heavier elements have been formed in star explosions. You are made of stardust.

If you drink water on an empty stomach, it can boost your metabolism by 30%.

If you toss a coin 100 times the probability that you will end up with exactly 50 heads and 50 tails is 7.959%

Bacteria are roughly 20-times smaller than human cells, while viruses are around 100-times smaller.

Viruses are not considered to be alive as they do not do all the 7 processes of life which are movement, respiration, sensitivity, nutrition, excretion, reproduction, and growth.

The largest black hole discovered in space so far is called TON 618. It is 66 billion times the size of our sun.

Muscles can only contract and can't push, which seems reasonable enough till you wonder how you can stick your tongue out.

You can't breathe and swallow at the same time.

In 2020 a study suggested people have more than 6,000 thoughts a day. The study examined 184 participants and used brain imaging to track new thoughts as they arrive. They found a median rate of 6.5 thoughts per minute.

Stents and catheters placed through veins into the heart are standard procedures these days. The technique was developed by Werner Forssman. There was widespread skepticism when he proposed the technique, so he performed it on himself. He gave himself a local anesthetic and inserted a catheter through his veins into his heart. He then went to the x ray department to prove what he had done. The life threatening stunt earned him the 1956 Nobel Prize for Medicine.

Golf balls have 300-500 dimples. These help reduce drag and allows the ball to fly further than a smooth ball would.

According to research by retailer Littlewoods four year old girls ask an average of 390 questions a day. That works out at about one every 2 minutes while the long suffering parent is awake.

It is just as well that sound does not travel through space. It has been estimated that the sun, from 93 million miles away, would make a sound of 100 decibels. That is about the same as a chainsaw, except the sun would keep making the noise for billions of years.

'Cosmic dust' falls to earth every day. It is generally small particles from meteorites, comets, and other solar bodies. It is estimated that 60 tons of cosmic dust falls every day.

The largest single organism on Earth is an Aspen grove in Utah. It is a woodland of 47,000 trees which are all clones which have grown from the same root system. It is spread out over 106 acres and is believed to be about 10,000 years old.

The largest earthquake recorded on Earth took place on May 22nd, 1960, in Southern Chile. It was measured at 9.5 on the Richter Scale.

The Richter Scale was devised by Charles Richter, an American seismologist. Each increase in a unit on the scale, e.g., 6 to 7, represents a tenfold increase in the magnitude of the earthquake.

A leech is perhaps the most peculiar creature. It has 32 brains, 2 hearts, 300 teeth grouped in 3 jaws and 5 pairs of eyes.

About 60,000 people die each year from rabies. Once the symptoms begin to show the disease is virtually 100% fatal.

Europa is one of the 92 known moons of Jupiter. It is believed that below the surface is a water ocean and is one of the main hopes for extra-terrestrial life in the solar system. NASA is sending a probe called Europa Clipper which has a planned launch date of October 2024. This would pave the way for a potential lander in the 2030s.

The human brain is split into two hemispheres, each of which takes on its own unique functions. The left side takes care of logic, numbers, and analytic thought, while the right side handles intuition, creativity, and imagination.

A windy day is a commonplace experience. What you are experiencing is a different pressure in two places and the air moving from the higher pressure to lower pressure.

Spaghettification really is a word. It describes what would happen to you if you were unfortunate enough to fall into a black hole. The gravity squeezes you while pulling you in the other direction and you would end up spaghetti shaped.

Ants that live in the Sahara Desert seem to find their way home despite the terrain looking very similar. Scientists believed they fixed on a landmark and counted their steps back to the nest. They tested this by putting some ants on stilts, so they took bigger steps, and found they overshot their nests as predicted.

The Asian moth Macrocilix Maia has a cunning camouflage strategy. It confuses potential predators because its wings look like two insects eating bird poo. It backs up this deception by having a very pungent odor.

The cane toad is an example of an attempted biological control that went spectacularly wrong. It was introduced in 1935 into Australia to eat beetles that were threatening sugar cane plantations. The toad proved a not very successful control of the target beetle as the beetles live at the top of the canes, and the toads can't climb. The toad has had a particularly marked effect on Australian biodiversity.

In 1972 the University of Stuttgart reported that one its students, Veronica Seider, had a vision that was 20 times better than average. She could identify people more than a mile away.

Swedish man Richard Handl was arrested in 2011 for trying to build a nuclear reactor in his home. He was doing it with some radioactive material he had salvaged. He wrote extensively on his blog about his experiments, so it is somewhat surprising that he was only arrested by Sweden's Radiation Authority when he asked them if it was legal. It wasn't. Mr Handl said he had always been interested in physics and chemistry and 'just wanted to see if it was possible to split atoms at home'.

Guam is the largest island in Micronesia, in the Pacific Ocean. After the Second World War the Brown Tree Snake was accidentally introduced after being a stowaway on a ship. As a result of this introduction several bird species have been driven to extinction.

Yucca moths play an important role in the survival of yucca plants. Without the yucca moth, the yucca plant would lose its only pollinator, and without the plant, the moth would lose its only food source. Each depends on the other for survival.

The Turing Test is a test of a computer, devised by Alan Turing. A person asks questions of the computer and another human and should be unable to distinguish which is the computer for the computer to pass the test.

The movie Toy Story 2 was accidentally deleted during development when one of the employees was trying to fix a simple problem but ended up deleting large chunks of the movie. The movie was only recovered because one of the staff members had a copy on their home computer.

The film had a budget of $90m and has worldwide takings of over $500 million.

Neanderthals are a species of humans that lived in Europe and Asia till about 40,000 years ago. DNA analysis has confirmed that Neanderthals interbred with modern humans. For Europeans and Asians an average of 2% of their DNA is from Neanderthals.

The Out of Africa Theory suggest that humans evolved in Africa and migrated from there about 60,000 to 100,000 years ago. All the different races in the world evolved since their migration from Africa. This theory is widely accepted by scientists.

Africans have no Neanderthal DNA, which would tend to support the Out of Africa Theory.

Human brains have become quite a lot smaller over the past 20,000 years. The Neanderthals had a 10% larger brain on average than we do.

The engineers working for Apple had made a prototype iPod for Steve Jobs, who examined it, before saying it was too big. The engineers said it was simply impossible to make it any smaller. Jobs took the prototype over to a fish tank he had in his office, and dropped it in. After it got to the bottom bubbles floated up. “Look” Jobs said, “Those are bubbles which means there is space in there. Make it smaller”.

According to some estimates there are twice as many squid as fish in the oceans.

Frogs can vomit, but not as we do. Rather unpleasantly they perform what is called a full gastric inversion. This means they don’t just eject the contents of their stomach but the entire stomach itself. They then wipe the offending substance away with their hands.

Sound takes 4.7 seconds to travel a mile. You can tell the approximate distance of lightening from you by counting the seconds from the flash to the sound of the thunder.

According to NASA an object which weighed 1,000kg at the South Pole would weigh 996.5kg at the equator. This 3.5kg loss is due to the centrifugal forces of the earth.

Europe and the US are physically moving away from each other due to something called continental drift. They are moving apart at an average of 1 inch per year.

The Mid Atlantic Ridge separates the North American plate and the European Plate and is where the two plates are separating. This underwater ridge forms the longest mountain range in the world.

The sun's diameter is 400.8 times bigger than the moon. By a remarkable coincidence the moon is 400 times closer to the earth than the sun which is why the moon covers the sun in a full eclipse.

The Passenger Pigeon was a species of pigeon that was endemic to North America. The pigeon migrated in enormous flocks and was once the most abundant bird in North America, numbering between 3 and 5 million. The bird was intensively hunted and the last one died in Cincinnati Zoo on September 1st, 1914.

On April 3rd, 1973, the first handheld cellular phone call was made by Motorola engineer Martin Cooper from Sixth Avenue in New York.

He called Joel Engel at his rival, Bell Industries, to inform him that Motorola had developed a functioning portable phone.

Dinosaurs were alive from about 240 million years ago to 65 million years ago, so they were about for 175 million years.

Recent discoveries have found evidence for feathered dinosaurs. The evidence suggests that birds evolved from dinosaurs.

The stegosaurus lived about 150 million years ago and weighed about 7 tons. Its brain weighed 2.8 oz.

You can get transparent solar panels which uses plain glass as a panel.

Human embryos have a tail that measures about one-sixth of the size of the embryo itself. As the embryo develops into a fetus, the tail is absorbed by the growing body.

There are planets floating around in space without a solar system. Scientists recently discovered up to 10 such free floating planets.

The moon was hot when it was formed and as it cooled it has shrunk by an estimated 600 feet.

Titan Arum is a lily which grows in Sumatra. It has a magnificent flower which can grow to 10 feet in height. The drawback is indicated in its name the Corpse Flower. It smells of rotting flesh. The deep red colour assists in the deception that it is a piece of meat to attract carcass eating insects to pollinate it.

It is possible to tell whether water is hot or cold from the sound it makes when it is poured. Water changes viscosity with temperature and the colder the water the higher the pitch is.

A neutrino is a particle of matter which is created by the process of fusion in the sun. They have a mass of close to zero and rarely react with normal matter. This is just as well as it is estimated that 100 trillion neutrinos pass through your body every second.

The Portuguese Man o' War, who's tentacles are highly toxic, is a dangerous species of jellyfish. It is estimated to be responsible for 20-40 deaths in the Philippines alone. The Portuguese Man o'War doesn't have a brain but does have 20 simple eyes.

The Blanket Octopus is immune to the venomous Portuguese Man o'War and rips off its tentacles and uses them for offensive and defensive purposes. The Blanket Octopus has 9 brains and is considered very intelligent.

The female Blanket Octopus may reach 2 metres in length, whereas the males are 2.4 cm. This is one of the most extreme differences between male and female of any animal.

The IgNobel Awards is a parody of the Nobel Prize and have been made since 1991 for research that 'first make people laugh, and then make them think'.

Among the 2022 IgNobel Awards were... the Biology Award went to a group studying how constipation affects the mating habits of scorpions. The Engineering Award went to a group trying to discover the most efficient way for people to use their fingers when turning a knob. The Physics Award went to a group trying to learn how ducklings swim in formation. The

Engineering Safety Award went to a man who developed a moose crash test dummy.

Justin O. Schmidt was an American entomologist who developed the Schmidt Pain Index for insect bites. To develop this index, he allowed himself to be stung hundreds of times. He was awarded an IgNobel prize in 2015.

The Bullet Ant scores the highest in the Schmidt Pain Index. According to Justin O. Schmidt, the pain is like "Walking over flaming charcoal with a three inch nail embedded in your heel". Some victims have compared the pain to being shot, hence the name of the insect. It is described as causing "waves of burning, throbbing, all-consuming pain that continues unabated for up to 24 hours".

Roman concrete is stronger than its modern equivalent which is why so many Roman structures have survived to this day.

Lungfish are an ancient group of fishes that can breathe air. The have gills but when the water quality becomes poor, as it does in periods of severe drought, they can breathe air.

Cows are more dangerous than sharks. Sharks kill about 5 people a year on average, while cows kill about 20. Perhaps sharks need better a better agent.

The Russian space probe Venera 9 was the first to take pictures on the extremely hostile Venus surface due to the searing heat and crushing pressure. The lander took pictures with one of the two cameras on board. The camera lasted 53 minutes.

An extremophile is a thing. It is a microorganism that lives in conditions of extreme temperature, acidity, alkalinity, or chemical concentration.

Tardigrades are extremophiles. Tardigrades can go into a dormant state for years in which they lose 99% of their body's water content. They have been boiled, sent into space and frozen to near absolute zero and survived. They are not immortal but are certainly tough.

In 1964 Doug Engelbart developed the first computer mouse. It was made of wood.

The Earth came about 4.5 billion years ago. Shortly after this it is an accepted theory that the Moon came about after a large object crashed into the Earth. The object has been named Theia which disintegrated on impact. The resulting debris coalesced with that from Earth to form the Moon.

Apple seed contains cyanide. Each seed contains 0.49mg of cyanide compounds. Don't worry this is a long way off enough to cause you a problem even if you ate them.

The fastest muscle of any animal belongs to the Giant Palm Salamander which comes from Central America. Specifically, it can fully extend its tongue in 7 thousandth of a second. That is 50 times faster than a blink of your eye.

The Earth is a giant magnet. The Earth's inner core is made of solid iron, surrounded by liquid iron. Variations in temperature and density create currents in this iron, which in turn produce electrical currents. These currents combine to create a magnetic field. This magnetic field protects us from harmful solar radiation.

The mourning gecko is native to the Indian and Pacific Oceans. There are no male mourning geckos as they don't need them to reproduce.

The auroras are colorful light displays and happen when solar particles collide with the atmosphere. Auroras have also been observed on Jupiter, Saturn, Uranus, and Neptune. The largest moon, Ganymede, also has auroral displays.

Bees have hairs on their eyes. It is believed that the hairs detect wind direction so help them to navigate in windy conditions.

A single bee will produce about 1% of a tablespoon of honey in a day. That means you will need about 3,500 bees to produce one jar of honey.

Although Saturn is the second largest planet after Jupiter it is also the lightest. If you could find a bathtub large enough to put Saturn in, you would find that it floated.

Owls have specialized feathers where the edges protrude out to dissipate airflow and eliminate sound. If an owl flies past, you will find that it flies silently. This means that they have the element of surprise which makes them deadly hunters.

Mercury is the closest planet to the sun, but Venus is the hottest. This is because Venus has had what is called a runaway greenhouse effect and has a very thick layer of carbon dioxide. This prevents heat from the sun escaping. The temperature on Venus is 465° Celsius which is enough to melt lead.

In 2017, Adidas sold over 1 million pairs of shoes made from recycled ocean plastic, each pair taking 11 plastic bottles to make.

More tornadoes occur in the UK per square mile than any other country in the world.

Bagheera Kiplingi is a species of jumping spider from Central America. It is unusual in that it is the world's only known herbivorous spider.

When you rub your eyes do you get flashes of colored light? There is a name for this light. They are called phosphenes.

While you are busy with your eyes if you shut your eyes tight shut you see a color. It is a bit lighter than black. Well, that color has a name too. It is called eigengrau.

Mount St Helens is an active volcano in the state of Washington. It had been inactive for over 100 years till it blew its top on May 18th, 1980. The eruption killed 57 people and it was the largest terrestrial landslide in recorded history. The total avalanche was 2.5 cubic kilometres of material.

You can start a sentence without necessarily knowing where it will end, or only a vague idea in your head. Despite this you can still finish the sentence and make perfect sense.

Aoccdrnig to a rscheearch at Cmabrigde Uinervtisy, it deosn't mttaer in waht oredr the ltteers in a wrod are, the olny iprmoetnt tihng is taht the frist and lsat ltteer be at the rghit pclae. The rset can be a toatl mses and you can sitll raed it wouthit porbelm. Tihs is bcuseae the huamn mnid deos not raed ervey lteter by istlef, but the wrod as a wlohe.

There is a popular myth that we use only 10% of our brains. It is wrong. Brain scans clearly show that we use most of our brain most of the time, even when we're sleeping.

Escape velocity is the minimum velocity needed to leave the Earth without any risk of falling back. The escape velocity from earth is 11.18 kilometres a second. If you happened to be on the surface of the sun (not advised) then the escape velocity would be 617.5 kilometres a second.

The acceleration due to gravity is measured in metres per second per second. On Earth this is 9.8 metres. On the moon it is 1.7 metres and if you are still on the sun, it is 293 metres.

When fleas jump, they accelerate faster than a space shuttle. In fact, more than 20 times faster. Due to their size and the force used to jump those great distances, their acceleration is approximately 100 times the force of gravity. They are said to reach 3 inches in a millisecond.

When you pull on a rope what you are doing at the atomic level is pulling the atoms you are holding closer to you. They in turn pull the atoms closest to them, and so on, till they pull on the atoms at the end of the rope.

Thermal cameras detect the heat lost by a subject as infrared, but polar bears are great at conserving heat which makes them difficult to detect using infra-red. The bears have a thick layer of blubber under their skin. They also have a dense fur which enables them to survive the freezing Artic temperatures.

It is impossible for humans to taste food without saliva. There are receptors on our taste buds that distinguish the taste of substances once they have begun to react or dissolve in the liquid of our saliva. This is a chemical reaction which the taste buds on our tongue detect.

If you leave the refrigerator open it does not cool the room down. In fact, it does the opposite and warms it up. The fridge is still extracting heat from air but is pumping it straight back into the room so there is no net cooling effect. The only thing that will happen is that the fridge motor will be going constantly and produce heat into the room.

A person who weighs 200 pounds on Earth would weigh just 76 pounds on Mars.

Dogs can be trained to smell cancer and can be an effective early diagnosis technique. A study found that they sniff out lung cancer with 96% accuracy and breast cancer with 98% accuracy.

The mountain top that is furthest from the center of the earth is not, as you might think, Mt Everest. It is Chimborazo in Ecuador which is a dormant volcano. Its height is 20,548 feet, which is a lot less than Mt Everest, but when the bulge in the Earth around the equator is considered, it is further away from the center.

It is often said that a goldfish has a memory of 20 seconds. However, anyone who has fed goldfish will know that the fish will remember when a regular feed time is.

Stromatolites, which are layered formations created by microorganisms, are the oldest known fossils. They are thought to be 3.5 billion years old. They can still be found living in salty lagoons to this day.

Blushing is an automatic sensory reaction only experienced by humans. Blushing gives a signal of our emotions to other people. This can be a powerful non-verbal cue which builds relationships.

Gregor Mendel, an Austrian biologist, is known as the father of modern genetics. His paper published in 1866 had little impact at the time. Before Mendel inheritance was thought to just be an averaging of parental characteristics. His genetic theory was first developed using pea plants.

The first vaccine was invented by Edward Jenner, a British scientist, in 1796. It was a smallpox vaccine. Smallpox was a particularly deadly disease in Jenner's time and is estimated to have killed 10% of the global population. His key insight was that infection with cowpox, a similar but much less dangerous disease, protected people against smallpox. He demonstrated that inoculation with cowpox from person to person protected against smallpox.

The Palmar Grasp Reflex is a primitive and involuntary response found in the infants of humans and most primates. When an object, such as an adult finger is put in an infant's hand, they instinctively grasp it. It is believed to be an evolutionary development of tree living primates. It disappears in humans at about 6 months of age.

The gravitational field of a black hole is so strong that even light cannot escape from it. This makes them essentially invisible to the human eye, which is why they are called black holes. They can be detected because of the effects they have on nearby space and matter.

The first wheelbarrows were invented in China around 100 AD, during the Han dynasty.

Numbers are an invention, and it is believed that there is no innate ability to identify quantities. The University of Miami were researching an indigenous Amazonian tribe known as the Piraha. They had no words to describe any quantities and struggled as soon as there were four or more of something.

NASA's Helios 2 space probe was launched in 1976 to study the sun. It is the fastest man-made object ever. It set a record speed of 157,078 mph during the mission, which is about 43 miles per second.

Under perfect conditions light can travel about 1,000 metres (3,280 feet) into water. However, there is rarely much light beyond 200 metres (656 feet). This led scientists to believe the wrongly that there was no life beyond this depth in the ocean.

About 75% of stars in our Milky Way are red dwarfs.

Scientists presently believe that the universe is made of something called dark matter and dark energy. It is believed that dark energy makes up 68% of the total mass of the universe, with dark matter providing another 27% and the stuff that you and I can see a mere 5%. Even though dark energy and matter make up so much of the universe no one has yet managed to produce any.

Glossary

Absolute zero – *The lowest possible temperature which is minus 273.15 Celsius*

Amino acid – *A simple organic compound*

Asteroid – *A small rocky object that orbits the sun*

Atom – *The smallest particle of a chemical element*

Atomic clock – *Extremely accurate clock regulated by vibrations of atomic system*

Bacterium – *A single celled microorganism*

Billion – *One thousand millions*

Black hole – *A region of space with a gravitational field so strong that not even light can escape.*

Carbon dioxide – *Colorless gas, absorbed by plants in photosynthesis, and a greenhouse gas.*

Cell – *Smallest unit of an organism and microscopic.*

Chromosome – *A threadlike structure in the nucleus carrying genetic information in the form of genes*

Clone – *Organisms, or cells, which are genetically identical*

Dark energy – *A theoretical form of energy said to be most of the energy in the universe*

Dark matter – *A material that is postulated to exist in space*

Digestive system – *The system of organs for getting food into and out of the body.*

DNA – *The carrier of genetic information in chromosomes.*

Enzyme – *A substance produced by a living organism which acts as a catalyst to bring about a specific chemical reaction.*

Fission – *The splitting of atoms apart which is what is happening in nuclear reactors*

Fusion – *This occurs when two atoms are joined together to make a larger atom. It is happening inside the sun and releases a lot of energy.*

Galaxy – *A system of millions or billions of stars. Our galaxy is called the Milky Way*

Gamma ray – *A form of radiation given off during the radioactive decay of an atom*

Gestation period – *The period of time between conception and the birth of young.*

Half-life – *The time taken for a radioactive substance to fall to half its value during radioactive decay*

Infra-red – *A form of electromagnetic radiation.*

Interstellar space – *The area between stars*

Kevlar – *A high strength synthetic fiber*

Laser – *A device which emits an intense beam of light*

Light year – *The distance that light travels in a year.*

Malaria – *A serious infection spread by mosquitos*

Metabolism – *A set of chemical reactions which maintain life. For example, the conversion of energy in food to energy available to the organism*

Metamorphosis – *A biological process of change in the form of an animal such as a caterpillar becoming a butterfly*

Meteorite – *A solid object in outer space such as a comet or asteroid. Once it lands on the surface of a larger body it becomes a meteorite. If it burns in the atmosphere, it is a meteor*

Microbe – *A microorganism, especially a disease causing bacterium*

Milky Way – *Our galaxy*

Million – *One thousand thousands*

Millisecond – *One thousandth of a second*

Neuron – *Cells in the brain responsible for receiving and sending information to other cells*

Neutron star – *The collapsed core of a supergiant star*

Ozone – *A form of oxygen which is concentrated in a thin ozone layer which protects us from 98% of the harmful UV radiation from the sun*

Pandemic – *A widespread occurrence of a disease over a country or the world*

Parasite – *An organism that lives on or in another organism*

pH – *A number which expresses the acidity or alkalinity of a solution in which the number 7 is neutral*

Photosynthesis – *A process in green leaves that uses chlorophyll and sunlight to produce nutrients for the plant*
Plankton – *Is the name given to a collection of very small sea life that lives in the ocean*
Probability – *The chance of something happening. It is measured from 0 to 100% probability. If it is 0 the event is impossible, and 100% is certain*
Radioactive – *A substance is radioactive if it gives off energy and dangerous subatomic particles*
Red dwarf – *A small, old, and relatively cool star*
Red giant – *The later stage of a star's life when it becomes very large and bright*
Solar system – *A system of planets orbiting a sun*
Stem cells – *Stem cells are cells which can divide to produce more stem cells or other cells which make up the organs or tissue of the body*
Supernova – *A supernova is a cataclysmic explosion of a star at the end of its life*
Tectonic plates – *Are the large and slow moving plates that make up the surface of the earth and explain how continents move*

Terminal velocity – *The speed with which a freely falling object reaches when the air resistance prevents further acceleration*

Trillion – *One thousand million*

Tsunami – *A long, high wave caused by an earthquake or other disturbance*

Ultraviolet (UV) – *UV is a type of radiation that is beyond the visible spectrum*

Vacuum – *A space without any matter in it*

Velocity – *Speed in a general direction*

Venom – *A poisonous substance secreted by animals and often injected by biting or stinging*

Virus – *Tiny particles that cause disease in people and animals*

X ray – *A high energy form of radiation*

ONE LAST THING

If you have enjoyed this book, I would love you to write a review of it on Amazon. It is really useful feedback as well as untold encouragement to the author.

Any remarks are highly appreciated, so if you have any comments, or suggestions for improvements to this publication, or for other books, I would love to hear from you.

You can contact me at
Blueyonderbooks2@gmail.com

All your input is greatly valued, and the books have already been revised and improved as a result of helpful suggestions from readers.

Thank you.

Printed in Great Britain
by Amazon

31264009R00066